ITS NOT ABOUT THE KNOCKDOWN

A teen guide to winning the fight for your life

IAN J. HUMPHREY

ISBN-10: 1494253313
ISBN-13: 9781494253318

Library of Congress Control Number: 2013921741
CreateSpace Independent Publishing Platform
North Charleston, South Carolina

Edited by Sherry Londo-Thomas

Dedication

I dedicate this book to the following:
Anyone who has ever felt that life was not worth the fight.
I want you to know that you may be down, but you're not out!

To those who refused to give up on me, thank you.

To those who believed in me when I didn't believe in myself, thank you.

To my family and friends who did not judge me because of my past
but loved me for who I'd become—I love you!

To my beautiful wife and children:
I would not be the man I am today without all of you.

CONTENTS

INTRODUCTION

"Everyone has a plan until they get punched in the mouth."

-Mike Tyson

On February 11, 1990, James "Buster" Douglas stepped into a boxing ring with the most feared boxer on the planet, "Iron" Mike Tyson. Tyson was undefeated, and Douglas was the obvious underdog. By the time the first bell sounded, the odds had been set at 42 to 1.

Douglas held his own until the eighth round when Tyson landed a powerful uppercut that sent him to the canvas. Dazed, confused, and barely beating the 10 count, Douglass rose to his feet. Two rounds later the world would witness something that never had been seen; Buster Douglas landed an uppercut followed by a brutal combination that dropped Mike Tyson onto the canvas for the first time in his career. Unable to beat the referee's count, Tyson suffered his first defeat at the hands of a man no one believed stood a chance. On that day Buster Douglas proved to the world, but more importantly he proved to himself, that "It's not about the knock-down; it's about the getup!" It's about what you do after the knock-down that defines who you are.

Leading up to that fight, Buster Douglas had every reason to quit: He had lost his mother to a stroke just 23 days before the fight. Shortly after that he suffered another blow when his ex-girlfriend, the mother of his child, was diagnosed with a terminal illness. In spite of all of this, he remained undaunted. Even after he developed a major bout with the flu, just before the fight, he refused to delay going to Japan for the match of his life against "Iron" Mike Tyson. Instead, he used those obstacles to fuel his hunger to defeat a man the world believed could not be defeated.

What obstacles do you face in your life that seem unbeatable? What setbacks have you experienced that made you want to throw in the towel and give up? Can *you* take those setbacks and use them to fuel your success as Buster Douglas did? Of course, you can!

If you have ever had days where you felt as though you wanted to give up, then this book is for you. If you've ever felt alone and that no one cared, then this book is for you. If deep down you really want more out of life, but you're confused and unsure how to get those things, **continue reading**, because this book is for **you**!

No matter how many times you've been told, "You're not smart enough! You're not skinny enough!" or "You're not good enough!" let me tell you this: *Yes you are*! You are all that and a bag of *Takis*.

But you must work on building up your belief. You have a Buster Douglas in you who is ready to beat the odds!

As you read this book, make sure you have a pencil available. This will serve as your personal journal to success!

Take a minute and ask yourself the following questions:

1. What is it that will make you say, "No matter what, I *can* and I *will* succeed?"
2. What is it that will motivate you to rise off the canvas after life has knocked you down?
3. What is it that is so important, you will change your life and stop your self-destructive behavior to achieve the success you desire and deserve?
4. What would you do with your life if you knew you could not fail?

Believe me when I tell you nothing gets your attention like hearing a judge say, "This court finds you guilty of armed robbery and assault with a deadly weapon and sentences you to fifteen years in prison!" I can still hear those words today years after they were spoken. They are just as clear now as they were then.

I stood in that cold courtroom with my hands cuffed to my waist and my feet shackled together. I was alone—no family or friends. After sentencing, I shuffled out of the courtroom thinking, *my life is over!*

I was only 19 years old, and I believed I would spend the rest of my life in prison. If someone had told me that one day I would not only be released from prison but that I would go on to start a family, own a home, become the general manager of a successful business, be a youth mentor, and become a professional speaker, I would not have believed it.

I was released from prison after serving four years, and today I have all those things I mentioned and more.

I will not pretend that this was an easy journey; it's been a process with many ups and downs and highs and lows. It required me asking myself the same questions I have recommended to you. It also required me following a strict set of principles I created and followed while in prison and after my release. Although these principles are ever evolving, they are still crucial to my life.

I wrote this book for you, because I would like to take the things I have learned and share them with others. If they worked for me, they can work for you as well. I've titled this book after my motto: It's not about the knockdown. I believe that life is sometimes like a boxing match, throwing punches at you from all directions and sometimes knocking you flat on your back. Like a boxer, if you don't find a way to rise from the canvas life will count you out.

In this book, I will give you the principles on how to rise after life has knocked you down. Take these principles and apply them to your life. If you do, one day you too may feel like Buster Douglas when he beat the odds to become the heavy weight champion of the world.

Are you ready to rumble?

BE IAN-SPIRED.

ROUND ONE

NO EXCUSES

"You can't hold onto your past without holding back your future"

-Ian J. Humphrey

The first time my cell door shut behind me as a convicted felon, reality sank in. My cell was eight feet wide and twelve feet deep. I stared at a brick and mortar wall etched with the writings of inmates who had once shared that space. A stainless steel sink, toilet, and a steel bed frame that held a two-inch mattress furnished the cell. The emotion of being a failure hit me like a sledgehammer. My knees wobbled before I collapsed onto the cold painted concrete floor. An uncontrollable flow of tears streamed from my eyes as I accepted that it would be a while before I stepped foot outside of the barbed wire fences or looked into the eyes of the people who meant so much to me.

As I lay on the floor, the words of my victim's daughter echoed in my mind: "You took my superman away." The brave little girl, only eight years old, looked at me and told me how I ruined the image she had of her father. I also heard other voices in my head like the voice of my foster mother, Ms. Alexander. She would often open the closet door where she'd locked me inside, and, in between her kicks and punches, she would look down at me and say, "You're stupid, and you ain't neva gone amount to much!" I heard the voices of family members that told me I would one day end up like my father, a career criminal who died in prison.

As I drifted off to sleep, curled up on the cold floor, I continued to hear those voices and concluded that everyone was right about me.

The next morning I woke up to the screaming voice of a prison guard: "Get the Fuck up--you're late for count!" *Where was I?*

Still confused, I jumped up. As my eyes regained focus, I quickly realized this was not a dream.

After all inmates were accounted for, I sat down on my bed, which wasn't any more comfortable than the cold floor. I thought about my life: How had I allowed myself to stray so far from the straight and narrow? It didn't take long for me to answer the same way so many other offenders had: "This isn't my fault!" I sat and thought about all the excuses and reasons I had to fail.

- I was born under very violent circumstances: My mother had argued with a neighbor earlier in the day. As my mom, seven months pregnant, walked up a flight of stairs, she didn't see the neighbor standing above her holding a pot of boiling water. As she made her way up the steps, the neighbor dumped scalding water all over her, sending my mom tumbling back down the stairs and into premature labor. That's how I entered this world.

- My mother received second and third degree burns over 25% of her body. Her injuries were so severe that she had a difficult time caring for me once we were released from the hospital. To help Mom recover from the accident, the doctor prescribed powerful medication so she could cope with the pain. Since my father was not present, friends and family took me in while she recuperated.

- At the age of three, during a brief stay with my mother, I went through her purse and found her pain medication and swallowed its contents. On the way to the hospital, my heart stopped multiple times. Eventually, I went into a coma.

- That accident led the state of California to declare my mother an unfit parent, and she lost custody of me. I was placed in a foster home where I remained for six years.

- Shortly after I arrived at my foster home, my foster mother began locking me inside a dark closet. While living in the home, I was abused mentally, physically, and sexually.

- At age nine, after a long court battle, my maternal grandmother was granted full custody of me. Seeing her driving up the street in a lime green Oldsmobile was one of my happiest memories. While living with my grandmother, I held on to the hope of knowing my mom was battling the court system to regain custody of me. To be close to me,

9

Mom rented a house near my grandmother's. After school, I would run to her house, and, instead of starting my homework, we would talk about becoming a family again. I wanted nothing more than to one day live with my mother.

- However, before any of those hopes and dreams became real, my mother passed away. I will never forget that day: I was asleep on the living room floor when someone banged on the metal security door. My grandmother jumped up and ran to answer it. The person at the door screamed frantically, "Mrs. Howell, wake up! Come quick!" I pretended to be asleep, but I recognized the voice of my mother's roommate. What she said next would set me on a path of destruction.

"It's Ruth! I can't wake her up! I think she's dead!"

That's how I found out that I would never hug my mom again. I struggled to remember if I had told her how much I loved her.

After I got dressed, I was ushered past the waiting ambulance into my aunt's car and taken away.

- The premature death of my mom was a knockdown blow for me. From day one, life had thrown its best punches, but I took those shots in stride, determined to stand and fight. However, the loss of my mom was too much for me to take, and I hit the canvas. I gave up.

Believing I was born to die, I drifted through life like a ship lost at sea. I had no vision and no hope. I surrounded myself with others that also had no vision and were hopeless. School was no longer important to me. I no longer cared whether I lived or died. I began committing petty crimes like stealing from stores. This gradually escalated to stealing cars and breaking into houses. Finally, it culminated with me sitting in a prison cell contemplating my future, making excuses, and blaming others for my situation.

It was much easier for me to play the blame game. However, if you desire more out of life, you will have to ask yourself the same question I was forced to ask myself: Who is the person that is holding you back? The answer stared at me every time I looked into the dull stainless steel mirror. I was responsible. The energy I had wasted blaming others was energy that could have been used to achieve my goals.

EXERCISE

Is there something in life that you desire to have one day?

_____

What do you want to be when you grow up?

_____

What obstacles have you faced that have caused you to veer off course, believing the things you want in life are impossible?

_____

When you look at your life and where you are, do you feel as though you could achieve more?

Yes_____

No_____

What's holding you back? Let's begin to change that by following these steps:

1. At the top of a blank piece of paper, write what you want to become when you are older. Beneath what you have written, write down why.
2. Skip a few lines, and write all of the things that have or will prevent you from achieving what you have written at the top of your paper.
3. Next, fold the paper to cover up everything except the goal at the top of the paper.
4. You should now see your goal and a blank space. Use that space to write the benefits of accomplishing your goal and what you can do to succeed. If you can only think of one reason, that's ok—write it down.

When you have a goal, the only thing that matters is the goal and how you plan to reach it. If you have 50 to 100 excuses why you haven't or can't achieve your goal and only one reason why you should, then focus on that one reason and not on the excuses.

Make copies of the paper and hang it up in places where it's highly visible. That way it's always on your mind. At the end of each day ask yourself this question: Did I do something today to get me closer to reaching my goal?

Writing your goals down is the first step to achieving them. At one time goal setting and achieving those goals were foreign to me. It wasn't until I was in prison that someone suggested I write out what I wanted to accomplish in life and why. I took that advice, and I have been writing and achieving success ever since.

The first time I performed this exercise, I wrote that I wanted to get out of prison and beat the odds by staying out! Since my release, I've done exactly that. Whatever you have written down, you can accomplish it!

MR. CHARLES LYLES

Change did not come quickly for me, because I was so focused on surviving prison. I took on the hard persona that many prisoners adopt. You know, the don't-mess-with-me-I'm-crazy persona. This landed me in solitary confinement for challenging the rules, fighting, and other negative behaviors. During my first year in prison, I was in solitary confinement for at least 6 of those 12 months.

Since my crime was violent, I was required to attend anger management classes. The teacher conducting class was Charles Lyles. He was an ex-marine from Detroit. He stood 6'2, was very slender, and soft-spoken. However, he carried himself in a way that exuded confidence. When I looked at him, I had the feeling he had seen things in his lifetime that I had only read about.

For some reason Mr. Lyles saw something in me. He would always stop me to say something positive or just ask, "Hey, Mr. Humphrey, how are you doing?" Every time I landed in solitary confinement, Mr. Lyles would visit me in my cell. He'd look at me through the small unbreakable window and ask, "What are you going to do when you get out of solitary?" or "What are you going to do to change your life?" Although I rarely answered, he'd ask anyway. When I did answer, I repeated my well-rehearsed excuses: "The world is against me. Everyone was right about me anyway; so, why should I try?" However, Mr. Lyles was not wavered by my rough exterior, and he continued asking about what my life was like before prison.

Every time I made a mistake he was there to encourage me. "This is only temporary," he'd always say.

Finally, one day there was a fight that broke out on the basketball court, and I landed in solitary confinement again. I sat in my cell with stitches in my lip, thought about what a failure I had become, and how unfair life had been to me.

I knew it was only a matter of time before Mr. Lyles heard about the fight and made his way to check on me.

When he finally arrived, he stood outside of my cell door and stared at me as though he were deep in thought. I felt badly, because I knew he wanted me to succeed, and I felt as though I had let him down again. I stared at the wall, ignoring him but waiting for his usual motivational pep talk. This time it never came. Instead I heard him ask the correctional officer to open my cell. This was not normal, and I was unable to hide my surprise as he walked in. There was no small talk, he simply walked up to me, looked me square in the face, and said, "Mr. Humphrey, prison doesn't have to be your life. You are capable of getting out of here and doing great things." He nodded his head as he spoke as though agreeing with himself. He took a long pause, and he continued looking at me as if he were trying to read my mind. He turned, took a few steps towards the door, stopped, turned back to me, and simply said, almost in a whisper, "I believe in you!" He then walked out.

Had he stood there for another minute, he would have seen my eyes overflow with tears as those four words resonated with me. That was the first time anyone had ever said that to me. Mr. Lyles had finally gotten through, and in that moment, I knew he cared.

I stood up, walked to the stainless steel mirror, looked myself in the eyes, and repeated the words of Mr. Lyles: "He believes in you, and you can get out of here and do great things."

This was the powerful moment that turned my life around.

The next morning I felt better than I had in a very long time. After washing my face, I looked at myself in the mirror and repeated the words Mr. Lyles had spoken to me the night before. I made it my ritual, repeating his words to myself over and over. I did this daily until his words became my words as I began to believe in myself.

When I looked at myself in that mirror, I knew I was looking at the only person who could change my life. I faced the fact that it wasn't anyone's fault but mine that I had ended up in prison. I knew the only way I could change was to own up to my mistakes, and stop making excuses for being a failure.

My first night in prison I thought about every reason I had to fail: I was born without much chance of surviving, almost dying after swallowing my mom's medication, the abuse I suffered while in the foster care system, the loss of my mother, and never having a father or positive role model in my life. Today, I realize that those were simply excuses I made for myself so that I wouldn't be responsible for where my life was headed.

The first step towards achieving greatness and getting up after life has knocked you down is to stop making excuses. Don't focus on the reason why you can't do something, but find the reason why you should. As long as you make excuses for not moving forward with your dreams, you have imprisoned yourself. You will begin to free yourself when you can look at your reflection and understand that you alone are the one standing in the way of your dreams. That is when you will start to gain ground on whatever it is you want to achieve.

EXERCISE

When you have someone who believes in *you,* you can accomplish anything you set out to do. Is there someone in your life who believes in you? Write their name(s) on the lines below.

1. _____

2. _____

3. _____

If you have a picture of this person(s), hang it in a place where you can see it. This is your *Mr. Lyles.* They believe in you and see things that you may not see in yourself. Trust and hold on to their belief until your belief in yourself kicks in, and it becomes your reality.

After my release from solitary confinement, I made it my mission to change my life. With the help of Mr. Lyles, I did exactly that.

What great things does this person believe you can do with your life? If you don't know, find a way to contact that person and ask him or her.

Look at the list below, and check off the great things you would like to accomplish one day.

The last lines are reserved for you to write in your own *great things* or the great things that your *Mr. /Mrs. Lyles* sees in you.

Earn a spot on a sports team	_____
Raise your G.P.A.	_____
Become a better friend	_____
Become a better student	_____
Learn a trade	_____
Get along better with family	_____
Graduate from high school	_____
Inspire and mentor others	_____
Obtain a college degree	_____
_____	_____
_____	_____
_____	_____
_____	_____

As you work to achieve the things on your list, when you find yourself making excuses as to why you aren't working on those goals, look at that picture and say, "**No excuses**; (Name) believes in me!"

"JUST DO IT!" "GIT 'ER DONE!"

For many people, making excuses is a habit. You may know someone that always has an excuse on the tip of his or her tongue. You know the type, the one who gets fouled during *every* missed shot.

The habit of making excuses can cause you to justify spending the rest of your life in your own prison cell.

Here are a few tips that can help with those bad habits. These are what I call *Take Action Tips.* Use these tips when excuses arise, and counter them by taking action! In this book, I will provide you with various methods of taking action. Stick with the one that works best for you.

1. Create deadlines for yourself. (Use the NOW and THEN Process™).

   □ If you've checked Raise My G.P.A. on the previous page, let's use that as an example.

   Below, you will find a line with the word *Now* written beneath it. On that line write down today's date. Next, find the line that says *Then*, and write down the latest possible date you wish to see a positive change in your G.P.A. An example is provided below.

June 2013   Raise G.P.A.   June 2023
Now   Then

Find a tutor.
Study an extra 20 minutes per day.

_____   _____

Now   Then

_____

_____

☐ Today's date (*Now*), or the date you write down, represents your commitment to change and gives you a clear day to begin.

☐ Your achievement date (*Then*) is your deadline. The space between the two is where you write down what you would like to achieve.

The lines beneath give you a place to write what you need to do between *Now and Then* to achieve your goal. This is your Plan of Action. Clearly defined written goals, with a deadline, will increase your chances of achieving success.

Now, make it your mission to use the Now and Then Process™ to define, and accomplish your goals on time.

MAKE THEM HAPPEN!

1. Develop routines
   - ☐ One way to make sure you accomplish the goal(s) you have set for yourself is to develop a routine. Example: Every day from 6:00 p.m.-7:00 p.m., I'm going to work on_____ (fill in the blank). No exceptions! Set aside predetermined times to work on your goals.
   - ☐ If you do this every day until it becomes a habit, you will increase your chances of accomplishing your goals.

2. Unstoppable Mentality
   - ☐ This means that achieving success is so important to you that you would do anything (legal of course) to accomplish it.

My first job out of prison was working for a pizza shop making $5.05 an hour. I worked nine hours a week. The picture of success I had painted before parole didn't have me covered in flour and tomato sauce, but there I was. Although I didn't enjoy the work, it was necessary at that time, and I performed that job as though I were making a million dollars a year. I worked as though I were the owner of the company. I arrived early and offered to stay late. This work ethic would help me when the time and opportunity came to move up within a company I worked for years later.

If you are currently working and would like to move up in the company, have patience. But prepare and be ready when the opportunity comes.

If you are working in a fast food restaurant, become the best you can be in that line of work. Do that job as though *you* owned the company. Make each meal as though you were making it for yourself! Your hard work will not go unnoticed, and this will open up more opportunities for you.

People use *excuses* to delay action. Those few examples I supplied for you are action-taking steps that yield results.

Another great example of the *Take Action Step* would be Nike's slogan: *Just Do It!* If you know you should be working out or studying for a test later in the week, and you're thinking, *I'll do it tomorrow,* find a mirror, look yourself in the eyes. Now, repeat the words that many top athletes have said to themselves when they didn't feel like running that last mile, shooting one more free throw, or taking that last pitch: *Just do it!*

Another slogan that screams **take action now** would be *Git 'er done!* This phrase, made famous by comedian Larry The Cable Guy, is to plumbers, mechanics, and roofers what *Just do it* is to Michael Jordan, Lebron James, or Dwayne Wade. When he doesn't feel like plunging one more toilet, changing one more tire, hammering one more nail, he just says, "Git 'er done!"

Okay, I'm sure you get the point. However, you will need these tools to push through the excuses so that you can accomplish the goals you set for yourself. It is important that you begin these practices *now;* so, when you feel as though you can't finish something, you will hear the words, "Just do it!" or "Git 'er done!"

My grandmother would often say, "Tomorrow isn't promised!" So, when I come up with excuses that delay taking action, I tell myself, "Tomorrow is not promised—do it now!"

EXERCISE

Do you have a slogan that pushes you when you find yourself making excuses? Write it down on the line below.

_____

Use your slogan to help you *"Git 'er done!"*

FROZEN BY WHAT-IFS

When I found out that my parole had been approved, I was overwhelmed with emotion. The thought of regaining my freedom, seeing my family and friends, and working on my future … so many thoughts ran through my mind. However, as the initial excitement faded, I became frozen by *what-ifs*, and my thoughts began to betray me. I had been incarcerated for more than four years. I was now a convicted felon.

> *What if* I can't find a job?
> *What if* they don't hire me after I check the box stating that I'd been convicted of a felony?
> *What if* I don't succeed?
> *What if* I get pulled over by the police?
> *What if* my parole is violated?
> *What if* ...

What-iffing can become an excuse to fail. By *what-iffing*, you are preparing yourself for the worst thing that could possibly happen. But why prepare yourself for the worst? Why begin your day on a negative note? Why even imagine that anything other than good things are headed your way?

Repeat the following to replace the *what-ifs* :

- I've got this!
- My future is bright and filled with promise.
- Failure is not an option for me. I will continue to press on until I find success.

HAVING FEAR IS NATURAL

I once had a tremendous fear of riding roller coasters. When we went to amusement parks as kids, I'd get excited about riding the biggest and scariest rides. My friends and I would run as fast as we could and jump in the long line. But as we neared the front of the line, something would happen to me. Deep down in my stomach fear would start to build. I would joke with my friends to fight it, but this never helped. As I neared the front of the line, fear left the pit of my stomach and made its way throughout my entire body. As soon as it was my turn to board the scariest roller coaster in the park, I would make an excuse to get out of the line. While my friends rode the roller coaster, I would think up a good reason why I got out of line at the last second. I never wanted anyone to know I was afraid.

I no longer fear riding roller coasters. I was able to conquer that fear by *taking action*. The action I took was *getting on the roller-coaster*. After boarding the ride, I quickly learned I could do it, and the ride wasn't as scary as I once believed.

Being released from prison was a lot like being in that amusement park. After my parole was finally approved, I felt that fear begin to build up in my stomach. As my release date neared, I felt the same fear make its way throughout my entire body.

WHAT WAS I AFRAID OF?

Like the roller coaster, I was afraid of the hype. While standing in line waiting, I could hear people who were on the ride screaming. As others got off, I overheard them saying, "That was the scariest ride ever!" Their words fueled my fear.

I had heard similar stories about being released from prison on parole: "It's going to be so hard! It's easier to just finish your sentence inside. Parole officers only want to send you back."

Having fear is natural. I would be dishonest if I said I wasn't afraid of starting over, afraid of the unknown, and afraid of failure. Many people have this fear, not just ex-cons. It's possible this fear may remain with you forever. But in spite of your fear, you must decide to face it head on by taking *action*. The action I took in dealing with my parole was to walk out of that prison and never return!

The following are a few tips to help you deal with fear. Remember the following statement: *The only thing that can conquer fear is action!*

Facing it head on is necessary if you are to go after your goals and live your dreams.

When fear or *what-ifs* set in, *take action*! I have provided a place below for you to write down any *what-ifs* that you currently have. As you get closer to your *Then* date, more *what-ifs* may begin to arise. Write them down as they occur.

WHAT-IFS

_____

_____

_____

_____

ACTION PLAN

- _____

- _____

- _____

- _____

- _____

- _____

- _____

Here are examples of action steps you can use:

- *Visualize yourself succeeding.*
  I am a professional speaker who is afraid to speak in public and to large crowds. I know this may sound crazy, but it's true. I conquer that fear by visualizing myself succeeding in front of my audience.

- *Call someone you know* (Your Mr. Lyles) and trust. This is someone that always has that word of encouragement that pushes you through your fear. I have a mentor that I can call at any time. I trust him enough to say, "I'm afraid" or "I'm losing hope." I know that he will provide me with the words to take action.

  Continue working on your action plan to develop new strategies to push through your fears and negative *what-ifs.*

START WHERE YOU ARE

As much as I would like to believe there is something special about me that allowed me to turn my life around, I know there isn't. Many inmates told me, "Hey, you're smarter than me" or "You knew how to read and write—I can't do those things." My all-time favorite is, "Mentally you must be stronger than I am." Excuses! I believe you have to start where you are.

Years ago I decided I wanted to join a gym. I went out and bought a pair of gloves, workout shoes, shorts, and a tank top. I walked into the gym, found a bench press, and, after placing a small amount of weight on the bar, I began to perform my exercise. After the first set, I sat up and looked at the other men who were also working out. Most of them were more muscular than I was. I was embarrassed and felt like the smallest man in the world. Eventually, I got up and left.

How had everyone else become so muscular, and I had not? They certainly weren't born that way. They had to start where they were and work from there.

I made the mistake of comparing myself to someone who had been putting in the work for months, perhaps even years, before I had decided to get started.

My second mistake was I believed they knew some special secret on growing muscles that I did not. Had I started where I was, worked hard, ate right, and stayed motivated, I would have seen increased muscle growth just as they had.

Here's another example of starting where you are: If a cook set out to prepare a meal that required 12 eggs but only found half of the needed amount in the refrigerator, what are his options? He could ask a neighbor to borrow the additional eggs, he could send someone to the grocery store to purchase them, or he could become so frustrated with the fact that he doesn't have what he needs that he tosses out the dish and gives up.

Since giving up is not an option for you, you would need to find a way to get the additional six eggs to complete your task.

For years I've wanted to write this book, but I kept telling myself, "How can you write a book? You don't have a degree. Yes, you graduated from high school, but it's not as if you aced any of your classes." I held off until one day I heard someone say, *"You have to go now! Don't wait until you get all your ducks in a row, because that will never happen!* After hearing those words, I was reminded that I needed to start where I was, and stop making excuses.

Perhaps there are things you wish to achieve in life, trying out for a sports team, going to college, owning a business, owning a home, improving your relationship with a friend or your parents. Achieving those things may seem impossible if you focus on how far you have to travel. Start where you are, and focus on working towards your goal. Remember that no matter how slow your progress, it is still progress!

A Journey of 1000 miles begins with one step. -Lao-tzu, Chinese philosopher

START SNITCHING

What if you could change the negative connotation that is associated with the word *snitch*? Since you are reading this book, I'm guessing that there are areas in your life that you would like to change or improve. If you believe that it's possible to set goals and create a plan to achieve those goals, then you can be successful.

One of the definitions for *snitch* is to inform. Inform means to make aware of something.

Start snitching doesn't mean that you run and tell the world something that you've witnessed. It means that when it comes to the things you want to achieve in your life, you must inform as many people as possible (Make sure they are people you trust.). If it is your intention to be a starter on the football team or raise your GPA, run and tell those who you trust. If it is your intention to lead a successful life after high school, tell someone. Tell anyone that you believe would like to see you succeed. You must speak your goals into reality. *Inform someone today*!

FIND AN ACCOUNTABILITY PARTNER

Informing others of your intention to succeed will help you eliminate excuses. Let's call this person who you will inform your accountability partner. Your accountability partner is the person who knows about the things you want to achieve—the person you will *snitch* to. *Remember,* it is important that this be someone you trust. This person will support you and call you out when you are doing things that are not helping you achieve your goals. Think about people you can *snitch* to.

Below, create a list of the names of these individuals. If you don't have any names to write down today, don't become discouraged; eventually, you will meet someone. To start the process, write down the names of one or more friends who have the same goal(s) of success. Write the names of teachers who have encouraged you and believed in you!

Decide who would be the best fit. Talk to that person and explain to him or her what you are trying to accomplish and why you have chosen them as a potential accountability partner. If they agree, sit down with this person and share your goals. If they also need an accountability partner, you can fill that role for them as well.

Next, create a pact to hold each other accountable for working towards those goals. You will be stronger as a team than if you travel this journey alone. Later, I will also give you advice on how you can put yourself in a position (networking) to meet people who can help you.

If you are ready today to start snitching, determine which goal you would like to tackle first.

Next, explain to your accountability partner what you need and how your success depends on things that you tell them. If they are up to the task, make a verbal agreement for a check-in time of once a month, once a week or maybe everyday. How often you check in will depend on your needs and what your accountability partner is willing to do. Check-ins are times when your accountability partner(s) will call you to find out how you're progressing and if you are remaining on task.

Create an accountability partner log to keep track of these meetings, and monitor whether you are making progress.

SNITCHES GET RICHES

Why is it important for you to have an accountability partner? It is important because snitches get riches! Once you begin to hold yourself accountable for where you are and surround yourself with people who are holding you accountable, your chances of success will improve.

All the things you want to achieve in life-- finding a job, making the starting squad, raising your GPA, going to college—are your riches. Together you and your accountability partner are about to get paid!

So, start snitching. Remember when it comes to your success, snitches get riches!

This is the end of round one. Please take time to back track and fill in the questions you did not answer. Make it a point to share those things you have taken away from this round with someone else.

NOTES

ROUND TWO
TAKE A CHANCE

"My fear of failure is no match for my desire."

Ian J. Humphrey

Show me successful people, and I will show you people that took a chance at some point in their lives. If you were to ask them if they were ever afraid to fail, I guarantee all of them would say that at some point, the thought crept into their minds.

What makes them different is this: *their fear of failure was no match for their desire to succeed.* These people knew that the only way to achieve success would be by taking the chance and going after that *thing* they wanted to accomplish.

Anytime you set out to achieve success, the chance of failure is always there. Remember this: your success depends on you taking chances in spite of your fear.

EXERCISE

Below, write the names of successful people you know or admire. On the line next to their names, write chances they may have taken to achieve their level of success.

_____   _____

_____   _____

_____   _____

_____   _____

_____   _____

Take a chance as though your life depended on it.

STEVE WILDER REFUSED TO DIE ...

May 2009, Steve Wilder was asleep in his basement when he awoke in the middle of the night unable to breathe; his air passage was swollen shut. Afraid to call an ambulance, believing he wouldn't be alive when they arrived, he decided to take his life in his own hands. He ran upstairs to his kitchen, grabbed a butcher knife, plunged it into his own neck, and gave himself a tracheotomy. Wilder said, "I got a knife, located it (his windpipe), pushed in, and blood went gush." He went on to say, "Blood was gushing out, but air was gushing in." When asked whether or not he was afraid, he said, "I was scared to death. I was thinking about dying."

When I first read this story I thought, *wow*! This man decided that if it was his day to die, he wasn't going to die waiting on an ambulance. He wasn't going to leave his life in someone else's hands. He took a chance on himself, and the payday he received was *life*!

Many people would have died standing by a window waiting for that ambulance to arrive to save them. Far too often people don't move forward in their lives; they are waiting for someone to show up and give them direction instead of taking that chance on themselves.

Like Steve Wilder, you will have to take a few chances in life if you're going to beat the odds and achieve the greatness that awaits you. It's not going to be easy, and there will be some fearful uncertainty. However, the chances you take may save you from living with regrets.

Many of the chances that I took while in prison (and after my release) saved my life both mentally and physically. As a child abuse survivor, I grew up with a distrust of people. However, while in prison I realized that I wasn't going to succeed without taking a chance. I took a chance by believing Mr. Lyles when he said, "You can get out of here and do great things." Believing him was mental.

There was a time when I wondered what Mr. Lyles wanted from me. I believed that he would eventually let me down and abandon me, because that was my experience. However, realizing that I could not get through prison successfully without help, I took a chance on Mr. Lyles and his belief in me. Slowly, I began to trust him and act on his advice.

I confided in him that deep down I wanted to succeed in life. The problem was I didn't know what success looked like for me. I had no clue on how to lay a foundation that would increase my chances of getting out of prison and staying out.

Earlier I wrote about Mr. Lyles speaking what I called *words of life* to me while I was in solitary confinement. I told you how he walked out of my cell that day, leaving behind the echo of his words. These words remain in my mind today. Mr. Lyles continued visiting me every day until I was finally allowed to return to the general population. During those visits, he usually had a question, quote, or advice.

Here are a few examples of how he was able to inspire me to want more for myself. These are tools you can use that will keep you mentally focused.

1. QUOTE: "Someone's opinion of you doesn't have to become your reality." –Les Brown.

Mr. Lyles would repeatedly quote a man I had never heard of, but soon the quote began to hit home with me.

In a conversation with Mr. Lyles I mentioned to him that as a young boy I believed going to prison was a passage into manhood. I believed that one day I would end up in prison, because that's what people told me: "You're going to be just like your father. (Remember, my father was a career criminal. He died in prison.) You're stupid and you ain't gone never amount to nothin'!" However, Mr. Lyles just looked at me and said, "Someone's opinion of you doesn't have to become your reality." That quote rang true for me then and continues to ring true today: *Someone's opinion of you doesn't have to become your reality.*

Every day before work, I read an inspirational quote and write my thoughts in my personal journal. This is a great way to start your day. You can do the same thing by downloading apps that will send positive quotes to your phone every day.

2. QUESTION: What are you going to do when you get out of here?

When Mr. Lyles would ask that question, I didn't know how to answer it. In the beginning, I gave the standard answer: "I want to get out of here and stay out!" In hindsight that answer wasn't much better than the inmates that talked about getting out and getting high as quickly as possible. My quick answer wasn't what he was looking for. What he was looking for would require me to take some time and really think about what I wanted for my life beyond my release: first from solitary confinement and finally from prison. He knew that my new life could not begin until I had answered that question for myself. The answer to his question required self-reflection. I had to seriously look at my life and paint a different picture for my future.

One of the things I was determined to do was prevent someone else from making the same mistakes I had. I thought the best way I could do this was by volunteering in schools and in my neighborhood and sharing my message of making right choices. I was intent on sharing all the lessons that Mr. Lyles had taught me about being responsible for my actions and believing in myself.

Growing up in L.A. I had what I call a *kamikaze mentality*. If you're familiar with the kamikaze pilots of World War II, then you know that many Japanese pilots were trained to make suicide crash attacks. So, it would be safe to assume that a soldier that had set out on a kamikaze mission had no plans for tomorrow knowing he was not going to see it.

I never planned for tomorrow, because I didn't believe it was promised to me. I lived in the moment, having as much fun as possible, because at any moment, like many of my friends, my life could end.

Not planning for tomorrow and not having a plan caused me to drift through life. You must take a chance and begin to prepare a plan for your life *starting now*. Having a kamikaze mentality will not lead to your success.

I didn't know it at the time, but when Mr. Lyles asked the question, "What are you going to do when you get out of here?" he was forcing me to plan for tomorrow. Planning for tomorrow gives you something to look forward to—it gives you something to work towards. It forces you to make plans and create goals. *Looking forward to tomorrow gives you a reason to live today!*

3. ADVICE: Mr. Lyles advised me to write down the things I wanted to achieve or obtain after my release. He often said, "Thinking about what you want is not enough. Write it down so you can see it every day."

I wrote a list of a few things I wanted and carried it around with me everywhere. It served as a constant reminder of what I had to look forward to. I can still remember what I wrote down:

1. I want to own a car that doesn't backfire.
2. I want to one day own a home.
3. I want to one day have a wife and family.
4. I want to become a man of character, honesty, and integrity.
5. I want to become wealthy.
6. I want a Persian cat.

That list was very basic. I wanted what I thought were very practical things. Except for the cat!

As a kid, I don't know why, but I believed that all wealthy people owned a Persian Cat, and because I knew I wanted to become wealthy, this cat would serve as a reminder of the wealth I would have one day.

Are you wondering whether or not I ever bought that cat? The answer is *no*! My son is allergic to cats. However, I did obtain everything else on my list. I wasn't able to obtain these things overnight, but having that list, seeing it and reading it every day, created a hunger in me that kept me working hard toward those things.

Today I have a new list that I'm working on, and, as I accomplish the things on it, I will add new items that will challenge me to continue to upgrade my life and standard of living. Every time I create a new list, I am taking another chance. However, I am always thinking about the payday of life.

The tools Mr. Lyles gave to me helped me change my way of thinking forever. Mentally, I am stronger, because I took a chance on him and ultimately on myself.

Below, I want you to answer this question:

What can you do right now to begin working towards your goals?

_____

_____

_____

_____

Also, create your own list that has a few things you hope to achieve and own one day. Keep this list close to you, and read it periodically. Use your list to remind yourself of what awaits you if you stick to these few steps.

CHANGING YOUR ENVIRONMENT

I can't tell you how many people I've witnessed who had parties thrown for them after their release from prison. These parties included balloons, food, drinks, welcome home banners, and a yard crowded with people.

Unfortunately, after the balloons had lost all of its helium, reality set in. Soon old friends were ready with invitations back to old stomping grounds where they'd spent most of their time leading unproductive lives.

Beware of individuals that celebrate the negative things in your life! You will find that negativity loves company! Take care to avoid people who invite you down a road that doesn't lead to your goals.

Accepting this invitation is a misstep you don't want to take. However, changing your environment can help you begin a new life for yourself. If you hang out after school at a certain spot, and negative, unproductive people also hang out there, change your location—find a new spot to hang out! If you have surrounded yourself with negative people at one school, and you don't believe you can avoid them, don't be afraid to ask your parents if it is possible for you to attend another school for a new start.

Nine months after I was released from prison, I was still on parole, depressed, and I felt like giving up. I was still tossing pizzas and searching for a better job. However, no one would take the chance and hire someone convicted of armed robbery and a violent assault. I began to believe that going back to prison was easier than my struggle with rejection, easier than asking another family member for a handout, or a place to sleep on their floor. I lost a lot of sleep contemplating my next move, but I continued holding on, if only barely.

One summer I received a phone call—it was an old friend of mine. After explaining my struggles to him and confiding how close I was to giving up, he suggested that I move to Colorado where he lived. He believed he could help me find a job. I had never been to Colorado, and I had never seen snow, but I knew I needed a change.

Moving to a state without family or friends was taking a chance, but it would give me an opportunity to start over. I told him I'd be in touch. After hanging up, I felt butterflies as I thought about packing up the few things I had and moving. I began saving my meager earnings from the pizza shop. To make more money I started mowing lawns and cleaning houses. It took one month for me to save up enough money to buy a winter coat, a one-way plane ticket, and convince my parole officer that a move to Colorado was exactly what I needed.

TAKE A CHANCE

When everything was in place, I called my friend and
headed to Colorado. I stepped off the plane in Decem
who I hadn't seen in more than three year, met me at the airport. We
embraced and headed to his car. It was the beginning of my new life.

As we pulled out of The Denver International Airport, I saw snow
for the first time. It was a very surreal moment for me, and I knew
I was going to have to make this change work. Going back to L.A.
was not an option. I only had a one-way plane ticket, and I had no
other choice than to stay, stick it out, and make the most of it.

After checking in with my new parole officer, I set my focus on
finding a job. My second week in Colorado, I was hired by a local super market to bag groceries for $6.50 an hour, forty hours
a week! The move was already paying off. I started working two
days later determined to become the best grocery bagger the state
of Colorado had ever seen.

Even though I was the new man on the job with no seniority, I believed
I could work my way up by outworking the other employees. I told the
other baggers that if they needed a day off, I would take their shifts.
It wasn't difficult to find people that wanted to stay home instead of
working. Very quickly I was working seven days a week. I loved life, I
had money in my pocket, a newfound freedom, and success!

I knew I would not get rich making $6.50 to sack groceries, but I made
it my mission to work harder than the employees that were being paid
more money. Eventually, I knew my hard work would pay off.

As a bagging clerk, my duties included bringing carts back inside the store, clearing the trashcans once an hour, and wiping down the checkstands where the groceries were scanned. Although, I was only required to remove trash and wipe certain areas, I would go to other areas and offer to take their garbage out since I was heading to the trash compactor anyway.

One such area was the delicatessen. I would wipe the glass case and chat with the employees that worked there. This was not my job, but I'd stop by every time and offer to do these things for them. I learned the names of each employee working in the deli department, and, over time, they all knew my name. I was not looking for anything in return—I was simply happy to be employed, and it was evident every day I showed up. I became known as the hardest working man in the grocery business.

Changing your environment gives you the opportunity to start all over again. When no one knows you, you can create the image you want to portray. As you begin to become a better you, you can leave everything negative behind. You can be that person of integrity that your new friends can trust and depend on.

HARD WORK PAYS OFF

Two months after arriving in Colorado, things were going well. I had found a second job at a retail store while still working hard for the grocery store. My parole officer was genuinely happy for me as I gained momentum.

Moving looked like the best chance I had ever taken. One afternoon while visiting the deli department and taking out their trash, a woman, who worked there, pulled me aside. She informed me that someone was leaving the department, and this person would need to be replaced. She explained that even though I had no seniority, everyone who worked in the deli agreed I would be the perfect person for the job. Having nothing to lose, I thought, *why not*!

I filled out an application that same day. I gathered relevant certificates I had earned while in prison and the food handler card I had received to work at the pizza parlor. I submitted my completed application package to the store manager the very next day. I never believed for an instant I stood a chance against the other applicants. Two weeks later I was called to the store manager's office.

He closed the door behind us. It was then that I saw my employee folder in his hand.

"Ian," he began, "I've received a lot of letters on your behalf from employees. You've obviously made an impact."

He listed the names of men and women who worked in the deli, stating that they thought very highly of me and believed I would be the best fit for the small department.

"I normally would not promote someone this quickly," the store manager continued, "but I'm going to take a chance and offer the deli position to you."

I sat there in disbelief; not sure what to do or say. The manager broke the silence.

"Well, do you accept the position?"

Unable to contain myself, I smiled and exclaimed, "Yes, I accept!"

"Ok, then. Let's discuss your pay. How does $10.75 sound to you?"

I thought to myself, *$10.75…that's more than four dollars over what I make now.* Fighting to keep my cool, I finally responded.

"Sir, I believe that will work."

This promotion meant instant benefits, a union job, and better pay! Wow! I walked out of the office feeling like I had hit the lottery.

Many people would later say how lucky I was to get that promotion so quickly. However, I believe when luck or opportunity comes your way, your part is to make sure you are prepared.

When I looked back on the process, I realized luck had less to do with it than showing up every day and working hard. I do not believe I would have received that promotion had it not been for the deli workers speaking on my behalf. However, had I not done all of the little things that weren't in my job description, no one in that department would have even known my name.

So, I ask you, what do you believe? Was it luck?

> *"Opportunity may knock more than once, but if you aren't pre-*
> *pared, it doesn't matter."*
> *-Ian J. Humphrey*

Begin today by asking yourself, "What can I do to better prepare for the many opportunities that await me?"

A C.E.O.'S MENTALITY

> *"Life is10% of what happens to you and 90% of how*
> *you respond to it." -Ken Brown*

No matter what you want to achieve in your life, being successful requires a certain state of mind. I call it The C.E.O. Mentality.

Do you know the difference between a C.E.O. Mentality and an Employee Mentality?

The C.E.O. Mentality is one that requires you to have a vision of where you are at this very moment and where you would like to be in one, five, or even ten years from now. It's a mentality that forces you to focus on your grind 24/7. Let me explain.

Sean "P. Diddy" Combs is the C.E.O. of Bad Boy Records. Everything begins and ends with him. Since it is his company, he is always working. He's looking for new talent to sign and new opportunities to increase the vision he has for his company. If you were to ask him, "When do you stop working?" I bet he would answer, "I never stop working! I wake up thinking about Bad Boy's success. When I go to bed, I dream about Bad Boy's success!" He has a vision that he can always see if his eyes are open or closed. That's the C.E.O.'s Mentality. You are always on the grind, looking for ways to legally increase your success and your quality of living.

An Employee Mentality is nothing like that of a C.E.O. It is exactly the opposite. An employee goes to work, does the job assigned to him or her. When they clock out at the end of their shift, they stop thinking about work. Instead of being productive, they pass time in ways that don't improve their quality of living. Those with an employee mentality are the clock watchers. They wait for the clock to say, "It's lunch time, break time, or time to go home." When they get to work, all they can think about is going home.

Is it possible to have and maintain a C.E.O. Mentality when you're flat broke and don't own your own company? Of course it is.

Men and women who possess the C.E.O Mentality are willing to start at the very bottom and earn their way to the top. They never become complacent with what they have or where they are in life. They are always looking to do more and become more. Sean "P. Diddy" Combs was not always the C.E.O. of a multi-million dollar company. He started by running errands for a record company. However, he worked hard and made it his mission to learn more about the business so that he could one day do his thing. His menial job didn't pay much, but what he learned by working hard was priceless.

You may have heard this saying: *It's not where you start; it's where you finish.* I believe that it's not where you start or finish, but it's what you do between the start and the finish. That is what determines your success.

Another example of the C.E.O. mentality is a young man that started off with nothing. His name is Ken Brown. You have probably never heard of him, but as a child he also had every excuse to choose a life of failure. His parents were only 13 and 14 when they had him. Their life was a struggle that included being evicted from their homes 10 times. But with his C.E.O. Mentality he quickly rose through the ranks of the food service industry. He went on to become one of the youngest African Americans to ever own his own McDonald's. Today he is worth millions. He is an example of working in a field that others frown upon.

People assume that because you're taking food orders you must not be very smart. I have heard many people say, "I would never work for a fast food place!" That's an Employee Mentality. Ken Brown worked for the fast food industry, but because he possessed the C.E.O. Mentality, he saw an entry level position only as a necessary stepping-stone to get him to his ultimate goal. He recognized that within every McDonalds Corporation someone occupied the upper management position. So, he made it his mission and sought ways to learn as much as he could about the industry with the goal in mind of one day owning his own business.

What do these two young men have in common? They both started off broke with simply an idea and a C.E.O.'s Mentality. As a result of that mentality they have now achieved success that many thought impossible. Not only is it possible for them, it is also possible for *you*! I want you to find a mirror and repeat these words, "If it's possible for them; it's possible for me!"

I attribute my success after my release from prison to having a C.E.O.'s Mentality and not an Employee's mentality.

Eventually, I left the grocery store business to take an entry-level position as a roofer. I had married and had started a family, and I wanted to have the freedom to be home on weekends, holidays, and attend my children's school functions. Unfortunately, the grocery business required me to work at times that would prevent me from being home as much as I wanted. My life had changed, and I chose to walk away. I had to take that chance to achieve my goal of being a good husband and being the father I never had.

My new roofing job was not easy. The summers were very hot, and, depending on where you live, it may snow or become very cold during winter months—you're always dealing with the elements. I recognized very quickly that this was not a job a man could do for the rest of his life. As a result, I looked for opportunities within the company to advance.

I started off working on a two-man crew with a foreman and a supervisor. The supervisor was in charge of making sure the foremen were keeping their crews on schedule. Most of the supervisors' days were spent driving to job sites, checking crews, taking measurements, and planning the start of new projects. I knew little about roofing, nor did I know how long it took to learn enough to fill a supervisor position, but it was on my radar.

The company also had a safety director. His job was to drive job sites and make sure crews were using their safety equipment and following company rules. His job also included transporting injured workers to and from their doctor appointments. This was a job I knew I could do right away. When the current safety supervisor quit to accept a position with the police force, I set an appointment with the owner of the company. During the appointment, I stood in his office and said, "Sir, I know you will soon need a new safety director. I'd like you to keep me in mind for that position." The owner knew I had not been there very long and chose his words carefully when telling me he appreciated me coming in, but I wasn't qualified.

I went back to roofing and one year later, after losing another safety director, I was back in the owner's office. Once again, he let me down politely, and I returned to my job.

I continued using my C.E.O.'s Mentality to find other opportunities within the company.

¿HABLAS ESPAÑOL?

Since most of the employees spoke Spanish, I knew as a supervisor or foreman I would need to learn Spanish. Time and time again I listened to my foreman complain about the difficulties he had communicating with Mexicans. He'd often said, "Why don't they learn English?" I never understood why the foreman, the person in charge of the crew, just didn't learn Spanish so he could communicate with his workers.

That was it! If I wanted to move up the ladder in the company, I needed to learn Spanish. By learning Spanish I'd have more value than the foreman or the supervisor who did not know how to speak the language. I felt strongly that by learning Spanish, it would guarantee my promotion.

I started right away by asking questions, "cómo que dice *ladder* in Español?" or "How do you say ladder in Spanish?" Then I would use that word all day long at every opportunity. I wrote every word down and kept the list with me.

At lunchtime, I would sit with the Spanish-speaking employees and listen to their conversations. While sitting with them, I also used words I had learned. I often said things incorrectly, and they laughed at me. But in the end I gained the respect of the guys; eventually, they began to help me learn. One year later I was a foreman with my own crew. Soon afterwards I became the only African American supervisor in the company. Later, I went on to become the General Manager of a new company that was started by the same owners

All of these things required me to take chances. Was I afraid? Of course. However, because I maintained a C.E.O.'s Mentality, it demanded that I continued working hard to find ways to move up.

¿Hablas Español? Do you speak Spanish?

WHAT IS YOUR VISION?

People confuse vision with eyesight—they are not the same. Not even close. Eyesight can be taken away from you but not your vision.

Vision is what Stevie Wonder and the late Ray Charles had while composing music. Ray Charles lost his eyesight as a child, and Stevie Wonder was born without sight. However, both men had a vision of what they wanted to create musically, and they accomplished it.

I often say that vision is what you see when your eyes are closed. It's what you see yourself doing tomorrow even though tomorrow has not yet arrived.

So I ask you again: what is your vision?

Using the word vision I have created a six-step process to help you get closer to achieving yours.

V. Variety Of Interest.

Being diverse in your interest can create unique opportunities for you to network with others.

When I was 11 years old, my uncle told me something I will never forget: "Make sure you listen to all types of music. Everyone loves music, and that will give you something in common with them."

Although I didn't know exactly what he meant at the time, I followed his advice. I listened to different radio stations like jazz, country, blues, and alternative music. What I discovered was this: Hip Hop and R&B weren't the only music I enjoyed. I discovered George Strait, Charlie Pride, Z.Z. Hill, and Clarence Carter. Also, I enjoyed The Goo Goo Dolls and The Smashing Pumpkins. These were all different genres of music, but they all had songs to which I could relate. This allowed me to begin conversations with just about anyone.

Here's an example: You are interviewing for a job and the person that is conducting the interview is listening to *Blue Skies* by George Strait. You can ask him or her, "Do you like George Strait? *Run* is one of my favorites (*Run* is a George Strait song.)! You have now created a connection with the interviewer and made yourself more memorable.

Too many times we identify ourselves by the things that other people tell us we should like or listen to. I once saw a T-shirt that read, *I am Hip Hop*! I asked the young man, "Why not, *I am music*?" His response was a long tirade laced with curse words that basically said all he listened to was Hip Hop, because he was gangster. Meanwhile, he was wearing skinny jeans and a pink shirt. There was nothing *gansta* about him. He was caught up in believing that's who he should be.

You don't want an I-am-hip-hop attitude, but an I-am-music attitude. That should also be your approach to life. Don't allow others to dictate what you should enjoy. Be open to new things. Don't let the fear of not fitting in hold you back.

I. Invest In Yourself.

The best investment you will ever make will be in yourself. You are never too young to invest in your future. That's what you're doing when you study for an exam.

Investing in yourself can be done simply by reading as many books as you possibly can on a variety of different topics. You may be pleasantly surprised when you read books you thought you had no interest in.

I once thought biographies were boring stories about dead people, but I had never read one. So, I didn't know if I'd like them or not. That attitude probably came from someone else and not me.

I was in the process of reading gangster books by Donald Goines and Iceberg Slim when my mentor, Mr. Charles Lyles, encouraged me to read a biography. He said, "How can you say you hate biographies if you've never read one?" I could not argue with that; so, I read the biography of Malcolm X, and I loved it. I learned things about him that I never knew. Things like his pilgrimage to Mecca and the effect it had on his life.

What Malcolm experienced changed his worldview. He no longer believed whites were exclusively evil, and he ended his call for black separatism. He discovered the power of Islam as a means to unity and self-respect. In his autobiography, he wrote, *The Holy City of Mecca had been the first time I had ever stood before the Creator of All and felt like a complete human being.* Malcolm X had found his purpose in life that we all are searching for.

I went on to read The Diary of a Young Girl, by Anne Frank. This was a story on survival. A young Jewish girl wrote in her diary while she and her family hid in an attic for two years to escape persecution from the Germans during World War II. I never would have thought I would have been interested in these books, but I was. By reading them, I learned, regardless of my initial thoughts or feelings, to give things a try.

What are some books you plan to read?

_____

_____

_____

_____

_____

Another way to invest in yourself is by having a willingness to work at any job available, or create work for yourself.

I have met several young kids that refuse to work at a fast food restaurant. Instead, they would rather just sit at home.

Recently, I paid a visit to my nephew who is serving a 16-year prison sentence. I asked, "Would you receive a certificate if you worked in the kitchen?"

"Yes," he said, "but I ain't working in no kitchen."

Many have this attitude and look down on the food service industry.

I previously mentioned Ken Brown. Remember his attitude? He saw the food service industry as an opportunity. It's about vision and seeing what the end of the road looks like.

I worked in our prison's kitchen for almost a year. The certificate I earned helped me land that job tossing pizzas. It further helped me gain the experience I needed to secure the deli position. Look at menial jobs as only a stepping-stone. You should never take the attitude that you are above certain types of work.

By the time I was released from prison, I had experience working in the metal shop, wood shop, kitchen, laundry, and general maintenance. I had no idea how or if I would ever use this knowledge. Whitney Young said it best: "It is better to be prepared for an opportunity and not have one, than to have an opportunity and not be prepared."

Working around dirty laundry was not a glamorous job. However, if the opportunity had presented itself, I would have used my certificate to secure a job on the outside doing laundry.

I used my knowledge of general maintenance to clean houses for single women and the elderly. By word of mouth, I was soon cleaning five houses per week. Again, cleaning houses was not something I ever saw myself doing, and I didn't enjoy it; however, it was an opportunity I had prepared for, and it put money in my pocket.

You can create jobs for yourself by offering to cut grass or shovel snow. It's not glamorous, but it's a job people will gladly pay someone else to do as long as they do a nice job.

Even if you don't see the need right now, you can take CPR and lifeguard classes. These come in handy when someone needs a babysitter or when the local pool needs a lifeguard.

S. Selling Yourself Short

Most people are told more about their limitations than their potential.

I will never forget Mr. Lyles saying, "Son, you can get out of here, and you can do great things. Prison doesn't have to be your life!"

Until that moment, I believed that prison was my destiny. I believed it was a passage to manhood. I mentioned earlier how I held on to this because that's what others told me from the time I was a little boy. I repeatedly heard how I would end up like my father; how I would never amount to much either. I was told this so much that I started to adopt a persona that ensured this would happen. By doing this, I sold myself short!

Anytime you aren't living up to your full potential, but living down to the expectations of others, you are selling yourself short. You rob yourself of a better life and more opportunities.

There are several things that contribute to people selling themselves short. **Perception without an interception** will cause this.

While growing up I witnessed drug deals, prostitution, and gang violence. Helicopters would shine their light into our home while searching for someone who had committed a crime in our neighborhood. This was all normal to me. My perception was this must happen everywhere. I didn't find out this was untrue until later in life.

Someone needed to step in and tell me the things I saw were wrong and should not be happening. I should have been told, "You can go to college, leave this neighborhood, and create a better life." That's the interception.

When someone disappeared or hadn't been seen for a while in our neighborhood, I never thought for an instant they had gone off to college. I automatically assumed they were in prison. That's why it was easy to believe the day would come for me to also head off to prison. I had sold myself short. Looking back, most of our neighborhood had sold itself short.

Lack of confidence can lead to people selling themselves short.

Like many children growing up in the city, I knew how to fight and defend myself. Older boys often challenged me to a fighting match, which I *had* to accept. Over time, I became good at fighting. This boosted my confidence so much that I'd fight just about anyone.

When it came to fighting and surviving, many of us possessed a confidence that was second to none. That confidence disappeared when placed in a classroom. We crumbled, because we lacked confidence. I felt more comfortable fighting in the streets than I did sitting in a classroom

A friend once said, "You must get comfortable being uncomfortable." This is true. If you are not comfortable doing certain things, it is probably because you haven't done them long enough to gain confidence. Most people quit at the first sign of discomfort. But if you stick with it, you will soon become comfortable with your new pursuit. That is when the magic of success happens.

Gaining confidence will help prevent you from selling yourself short.

I. Intentions

I once saw a movie where the father sat down with his daughter and her new boyfriend. The father was wearing his Marine Corp uniform and cleaning his revolver.

The father leaned over and said, "Son, what are your intentions with my daughter?"

"We're going to see a movie, and as soon as the movie is over, I'm bringing her home safely, sir."

The father smiled, and leaned back in his chair.

"Enjoy the movie," he said as he continued cleaning his pistol.

To achieve greatness, it is important to know your intentions. Whether you act in line with those intentions is totally up to *you*.

The day I was released on parole, my intention was to go to The International House Of Pancakes (IHOP). It was one of the first things I planned on doing. I even knew what I would order: a large stack of pancakes, bacon, extra sausage, and a fried egg with a tall class of orange juice. After my release, I did exactly that.

The second thing I knew I needed to start right away was rebuilding my life. I had outlined what that entailed. It looked something like this:

2. Get busy rebuilding your life.

- Check in with Parole Officer (PO).
- Begin mapping out places to apply for work.
- Each day find two new places to apply.
- Stay positive no matter what.

AND THE LIST WENT ON …

What are your intentions while in high school or while in college?

_____

_____

_____

We all know that sometimes good intentions go bad.

After my release, I easily could have done something other than what I had outlined. There were times when old friends tested my conviction to change. They would call and ask if I wanted to go to a party or hang out. I knew I had to stick with my intentions. I knew these distractions would occur, but I had mentally prepared for them before I was released. I had already pictured those old friends calling and stopping by. But in the picture I had created, I saw myself telling them I couldn't hang out.

Can you identify any potential pitfalls that could make your intentions go bad? Write those potential pitfalls below and the things you will do to avoid them. If you are unable to avoid them, write what you will do to get out of the situation.

*You may notice some things you write down already have been written earlier. That is okay—write them down anyway. This will help drive home your beliefs.

Potential pitfalls	Avoid by
-------------------	-------------------------------
-------------------	-------------------------------
-------------------	-------------------------------
-------------------	-------------------------------
-------------------	-------------------------------
-------------------	-------------------------------
-------------------	-------------------------------

O. Open your eyes to new opportunities.

Look around your school. Are there students who focus only on the negative: "The food here sucks! Our football team is horrible!" These students only see doom and gloom.

Are there others who are very intelligent, but have chosen to sit around and not make the most of their potential? It is a mistake for you to hang out with these under-achievers. Their negativity will cause *you* to miss out on opportunities.

For example: A teacher offers to stay late to help students to better understand an assignment. She's offering an opportunity to her class. However, your negative friend responds, "Staying after class? How lame!" You don't want to seem *lame*; so, you rethink whether or not you should take advantage of this opportunity to receive extra help.

By reading this book and writing in your journal, you are opening your eyes to new opportunities.

N. Never fear change.

Earlier I mentioned how a good friend said to me that I needed to get comfortable with being uncomfortable. My first response to her was, "What the hell are you talking about?" However, over the years, I have come to understand what she meant that day. Change is something that is necessary for success. We often fear it, because it's uncomfortable.

It is natural for us to fight change in an attempt to return to what we are accustomed to. As you pursue change, the discomfort will soon fade, and, before long, you will become comfortable with the very thing that once made you uncomfortable.

Have you ever been asked to take a detour from your normal route? Perhaps a familiar road was closed for reconstruction. How did you respond when you saw the orange sign that read, DETOUR

AHEAD or ROAD CLOSED? Did you panic because you thought you'd be late to your destination? Were you afraid you'd get lost?

I used those examples because I was that person! Taking the familiar route is safe, comfortable, and preferred.

What I learned from taking the road less traveled was that I noticed things that I hadn't before: restaurants and businesses I didn't know were there. Had I not taken this route I never would have seen those things.

Change is an opportunity to find new ways of doing things, things you may be interested in. It's a chance to challenge and stretch yourself to become the person you were truly meant to be.

When you hear the word change, you must condition yourself to think *opportunity*! Never fear change; embrace it.

EXERCISE

Take a moment and write down your vision. What do you see for yourself and your future in one year, three years, and seven years from now?

One year _____

Three years _____

Seven years _____

MY CHALLENGES TO YOU!

1) Make the choice right now to take some chances! It was Les Brown who said, "Most people aim too low, and they hit their mark." Take a chance, and aim high. You never know what could happen.

2) Decide now that, starting with tomorrow, you're going to do more; you're going to work harder than everyone else in your classroom and on your team. Every day is a competition, and every day you are competing for success.

3) Maintain a good attitude! Some people walk into their school daily believing that the odds are stacked against them. While others walk into that same school believing they are about to conquer the world and achieve the greatness they deserve. Whatever you are thinking when you walk into your school, you will be right.

This is the end of round two. Please take time to reflect on all of the things you have taken away from this round. Make it a point to share those things with someone else.

NOTES

ROUND THREE

CHECK YOUR CREW

Have you ever heard someone say, "I got in trouble because I was hanging around the wrong people?" How many people have you heard say, "I was the wrong person that they were hanging out with?"

I'm not going to say I got in trouble and sentenced to 15 years in prison because I was hanging out with the wrong people, nor will I say I was the wrong person. I will say this: there was a time in my life that I lacked the courage to speak up and speak out because I didn't want to be different.

When the crew I was hanging with suggested that we rob someone, I didn't have the courage to say, "No!" I didn't have the strength to speak up and say, "This is wrong, and we should not be doing this." or simply, "Let me out of the car—I don't want to be involved." I complied by remaining silent.

The night I committed the crime that sent me to prison began with my crew and me going to a club. When we left that night, I had no intention of committing a crime. I was tired and looking forward to going to bed. As we headed home, I dozed in and out of sleep until I heard the driver say, "Let's get this fool!" When I looked up, I could barely see the man through the darkness. Everyone in the car, including me, knew "Let's get this fool!" meant we were going to rob him.

When we pulled over into the shadows, thoughts of escaping the situation raced through my mind. To this day I don't know why they handed me the baseball bat. As I took it in my hands, I again dismissed thoughts of escape—I did not want to be the only one to *punk out*. Secretly, I hoped someone else would speak up, but as we walked towards the man, bat in hand, that never happened. With that bat, I broke the man's jaw, kneecap, and fractured his skull, almost killing him. While I was swinging the bat, someone else stole his personal belongings. That night changed many lives.

We were unaware that someone had watched us commit the crime. That person flagged down the police and reported us. The police quickly found us close to the scene and stopped to ask questions. During questioning, they noticed blood on one of our shirts. We were taken to the police station for more questioning, and I was later arrested and placed into custody.

I would not be released for more than four years. After swearing they would remain silent, my crew testified against me for a lighter sentence. In the end, when it comes down to you or them, most people want to save themselves. I do not hold anything against them for testifying against me. I know that in the end I am still responsible for my own actions. Over time, I realized that if I had had the courage to speak up, I would not have been in that situation. This adjustment in thinking was necessary for me to change my life, get out of prison, and stay out.

Many people have asked if I sought revenge on those who testified against me? The answer is NO! It was not anyone else's fault. I chose to commit a crime.

Please finish the following sentence: You are the company _____ _____ _____.

While growing up, I never quite understood what people meant when they said, "You are the company that you keep." Now I understand that they were telling me to check my crew. Avoid hanging around people that are going nowhere and taking you with them.

After sentencing, I had plenty of time to reflect on different scenarios. What if I had just ran? What if my boys hadn't testified against me? What if I had testified against them instead? Yes, I was *what-iffing*. The question I finally had to ask myself was this: *What if* I had checked my crew? I knew the guys I was hanging out with that night had bad reputations. They were all well known for all the wrong reasons. *What if* I had chosen to stay home and watch

T.V.? *What if* I had friends that were not drinking, smoking and looking for trouble to *get into*? *What if…*

During my incarceration, once I surrounded myself with offenders who had positive attitudes about their futures, I had the opportunity to answer those questions. However, finding people with the right mindset in prison was easier said than done.

It was not a problem to find a group of guys and have conversations about getting out. They discussed returning to old neighborhoods to get high, find old girlfriends, and return to the life they lived before their offenses. It was much more difficult to find a group of people whose intentions were not only to get out of prison, but to stay out and become successful. Since this type of group was challenging to find, I started a group on my own and called it Let's Rap.

We met a minimum of once a week. In those meetings, we discussed upcoming parole hearings and what needed to be done to improve someone's chance of being paroled. We practiced speaking and answering questions we thought the parole board would ask. We applied for the same classes and informed each other about available opportunities. We shared books and self-help material. Slowly, but surely, each member was eventually paroled.

At first, many people did not take us seriously and believed it was a phase that would soon pass. Other groups challenged us and attempted to derail our mission.

On one occasion someone, who claimed he belonged to the Crip street gang, angrily approached me and said, "You think you better than me, don't you?" I assured him that I didn't and that I was seeking to get out of prison and become successful. He laughed in my face and said, "You ain't gone stay out. You'll be back, because you're just like me!"

Later, he brought his group to the barbershop where I worked. When they attempted to enter the barbershop to jump me, a correctional officer saw the commotion and broke it up. After that incident, I was selective with whom I shared my thoughts about success.

The group we formed succeeded in avoiding trouble on the inside, and it provided me with a stepping-stone for success once I was released. I have kept in contact with a member from that group since my release. Remember the friend that called me and said he could get me a job in Colorado? He was in my success group. He was also my first accountability partner. We are still really good friends today. As a matter of fact, he has become like a brother to me. He was even in my wedding.

KAMIKAZE MENTALITY

Do you know someone who has a Kamikaze Mentality? Remember, that is someone who lives for today and not caring about the consequences of tomorrow. Checking your crew means avoiding those who think this way. It means you must surround yourself with people who are going somewhere with purpose, people who aren't seeking to destroy their life or, more importantly, your life. Find those who are making plans to excel and who desire to leave a positive mark on this earth. Participating in a group like the one I formed, Let's Rap, will give you the positive encouragement you need to succeed. You in turn can challenge and encourage others.

Exercise: If you formed your own success group, what would you call it? Are there people you know who would be great additions to your group? Write them below.

— —

Name of your success group

— —

— —

— —

— —

— —

Congratulations! After contacting these individuals, you will have your own success group.

PUSHERS AND POUTERS

In my senior year of high school, I received a phone call from my grandmother telling me my dad had gone back to prison once again. She explained that he had crashed his car while attempting to escape the store he had robbed. The car had been impounded and was available for release. She said the first person to get downtown and pay all applicable fees would own the car. My grandmother knew I didn't have a car, and she thought this would be a way for me to purchase one for a reasonable price.

Assuring me the car was not damaged much, she told me to call right away before someone else purchased it.

After calling the impound lot, I boarded a bus and took the three hundred dollars I needed to have the car released.

As I sat on the bus, hot and sweaty, I was excited and nervous as I thought about driving my shiny brand new car! I pictured myself listening to the radio and going to the car wash on weekends. In my mind, I saw every pretty girl in my school lining up to see my new car and asking to ride shotgun.

I couldn't wait. When I exited the bus, I didn't bother waiting for the next bus to come. Instead, I ran the three blocks to the impound lot. As I handed over the money, I was so excited that my hand shook.

As I followed the attendant through his lot, I was so close that had he stopped I would have bumped in to him.

Finally, he turned to me and said, "Here she is!" When I saw the rusty cream-colored 1963 Dodge Dart, I thought he was joking. The front end was smashed, and one of the headlamps hung loosely like an eyeball popped from its socket.

I opened the door and right away noticed the radio—it was an A.M. only, all transistor stereo. I was really disappointed that there was no place to play the M.C. Hammer cassette tape I had with me. I sat down in the drivers seat and felt the cracked leather scratching my leg. Looking through the windshield was difficult, because it was cracked from the accident. As I looked closer, I noticed that in the center of the spider web crack was a lock of hair. It undoubtedly had come from my father's head after it crashed the windshield.

I was very disappointed that it wasn't the shiny chick magnet I had imagined. But it was better than riding the bus!

As I drove the car off of the impound lot heading home, the tire on the damaged side wobbled and squeaked.

Weeks later, after fixing the tire and windshield, I began driving to school. The moment I pulled into the student parking lot, my friends laughed and called my car a *hoopty*. In other words, they thought my car was a piece of junk. But a funny thing happened after school; those same friends asked *me* for a ride home.

I guess I should have told them that the gas gauge was broken, and it was possible we would run out of gas. Sure enough we did. Right away two of my friends jumped out and began to help push the car to the nearest gas station while the other two ducked down in the backseat. They pouted and complained about their friends possibly seeing them in my car that was being pushed.

Starting today, what type of friends will you choose to surround yourself with? Pushers or pouters?

Pushers are friends who will give you a hand when you need it. Pouters are those who duck and hide and are nowhere to be found when times are tough.

AVOID NEGATIVE PEOPLE

Have you ever touched something that had glitter on it? In elementary school I crafted projects that involved glitter. Although I had a blast creating things for my grandmother, I didn't like the clean up, because glitter was difficult to remove. It would get all over your arms, face and legs. No matter how hard I scrubbed I could never remove it all. Even when I thought I had gotten it all off, a few days later someone would say, "Do you know you've got glitter on your face?"

Negativity is a lot like glitter; once it gets on you it's very difficult to get off. The only way to avoid having glitter stuck to you is to avoid it.

I bet you know or have seen people who only see what's negative about their lives or situation. Listening to their negativity can bring you down and cause you to become just like them. Avoid these people, and make sure they do not infiltrate your success group!

When I was younger I had a small Afro. My classmates thought there was nothing funnier than tossing a piece of Velcro into my perfectly picked out hair, because the Velcro always stuck.

Negativity is like getting Velcro caught in your Afro. You often had to cut it out in order to remove it.

To succeed, like with Velcro, you must cut the negative people out of your life. Negative people are saboteurs of success. They will do or say anything to derail your positive attitude. They do not want to see you succeed.

Remember the Titanic? It was a one of a kind *unsinkable ship*. Do you remember what happened to this unsinkable vessel? It sank!

Like the Titanic, you too are one of a kind and unsinkable. However, if your mind fills with negativity the way the Titanic filled with water, you too will find your way to the bottom.

So avoid it and steer clear!

Earlier I mentioned how my uncle taught me to listen to a variety of music so I could carry on a conversation with just about anyone. What I discovered while listening to different genres of music was the inspirational aspect. Music has the ability to inspire and motivate you to take action. It can also remind you to check your crew.

One such song that does this for me is a song by an old soul group called The Dramatics. I would be surprised if you've ever heard of them. They have a song titled, Hey You! Get Off My Mountain. This is a portion of the opening verse: *Hey you! Get off my mountain. Hey you! Get off my cloud. Hey you! Get off my mountain. You're just tryin' to bring me down.*

There are people in your life who will try to bring you down. They will attempt to get you to question your belief in yourself. If you have no one in your life right now like that, there probably will be a time when you will. When they arrive, you must have the strength and courage to repeat the words of The Dramatics: *Hey you! Get off my mountain. Hey you! Get off my cloud. Hey you! Get off my mountain. You're just tryin' to bring me down.*

Negative people come in all forms: an adult, a friend, a teammate, or even someone in your own family. But, no matter who they are, you must find the courage to push them off of your mountain or kick them off of your cloud. Negative people will definitely bring you down!

HOW DO YOU ELIMINATE NEGATIVE PEOPLE?

I'm often asked, "How do you eliminate negative people from your life?" Here's the simple secret: *There is power in numbers!* The voice of a negative person can be drowned out by the voices of a positive group! By forming the success group we discussed earlier, you will always have the numbers to defeat the negative individuals who will attempt to derail your success. By maintaining a positive attitude, negative people will scatter to find other negative people.

This is Checking Your Crew!

WHO'S YOUR CORNER MAN?

If you've ever seen a boxing match, you know that each fighter has a person in his corner known as the corner man. This is a term for a coach or teammate that is responsible for assisting a fighter during the length of a bout.

A few of their responsibilities include: placing the stool in the ring, taking out the fighter's mouthpiece, wiping their face, and giving them water. Additional duties are to remind their fighter to stick to the plan, or deviate from the original plan if it's not working. They provide encouragement and are also responsible for throwing in the towel or ending the bout if they believe the well-being of their fighter is in jeopardy. Ultimately, they are there to help the fighter succeed.

A boxing match can be won or lost by who the fighter allows in his corner. The same is true about life.

Imagine how successful a boxer would be if the person in their corner encouraged them to do something that could get him knocked out. They would not be successful at all. Picture this: The bell rings for you to come out of your corner to begin the next round. As your opponent hits you upside the head the person in your corner screams, "Ouch! Hey stupid, next time duck! My grandma would have seen that punch coming!"

Would you benefit from having this person on your team? Of course not. You would fire that person, because they did not have your best interest in mind.

The people you surround yourself with are your corner men. So, if you want to succeed, you must have the right person(s) in your corner. You cannot surround yourself with anyone who encourages negative behavior; that will get you knocked down or knocked out by life. Your corner man must provide you with encouragement and positive instruction, because they have *your* success in mind.

Often you can find a corner man that has been in your shoes, understands what you're going through, and what needs to happen to get you to where you want to go. A mentor is another name for a corner man. So, finding a mentor is as important to you as finding the right corner man is to a boxer.

Your mentor is the person you turn to for advice on obstacles you will face.

It's important that you trust this person's opinion, and they are not afraid to tell you the truth. Having the right mentor can help determine whether you succeed or fail.

Who are people you know at your school, church, or in your neighborhood who have your back and want you to achieve great things?

_____

_____

_____

_____

TROUBLE JUST SEEMS TO FIND ME!

While growing up trouble just seemed to find me! It didn't matter what day of the week it was or what I was doing; trouble just appeared out of nowhere!

For instance: One afternoon after school, I was walking down the street with my boys when a car passed by with another crew in it. They looked at us crazy, and we flipped them off. The car turned around, their crew jumped out of the car, and we fought in an empty parking lot. Fighting was our only option, right? What else could we have done? We weren't looking for trouble, but it certainly *found us.*

There was another time when we were celebrating my homeboy's birthday. We were riding around in a stolen car minding our own business. We weren't looking for any trouble, but it *found us.* The police pulled up beside us, saw the busted steering column, and attempted to pull us over. We jumped out of the car and ran.

I'll never forget the time we didn't have anything better to do; so, we went shoplifting and my boy Budha got caught.

Then there was the time when the police stopped my crew for just hanging out, minding our own business, and kicking it with an open container.

It never seemed to fail; whenever I was hanging out with my boys, trouble *found us.*

The crazy thing is after I learned to check my crew trouble stopped finding me. Since my release from prison, moving to Colorado, finding new friends, and surrounding myself with individuals who had goals, hopes and dreams, trouble has yet to find me!

The truth is that trouble doesn't just find anyone, and it certainly didn't just find my crew and me. We went looking for it. All it takes is for one person to say let's hang, and you have set a course that puts you at risk. Checking your crew eliminates the largest factor of trouble magically finding *you*.

There are a few quick and easy ways to determine if you need to check your crew.

YOU MIGHT NEED TO CHECK YOUR CREW IF:

- The only things you do with your friends involves drinking and smoking. *You might need to check your crew.*
- Your friends are walking in front of you, and all you see are boxers and butt cracks. *You might need to check your crew.*
- Your crew doesn't add anything meaningful, productive or valuable to your life. *You might need to check your crew.*
- Your friends aren't involved in some type of success group. *You might need to check your crew.*
- If you're the smartest person in your group, then *you might need to check your crew.*
- You're with friends that only discuss things they've done in the past, not what they're planning for their future. *You might need to check your crew.*
- Trouble seems to find you when you're hanging with your crew. *You might need to check your crew.*
- The actions of your crew have a negative impact on your future. *You definitely need to check your crew.*

I could go on with this, but you see the point. You could probably come up with a few examples of your own.

Below, I have listed a few ideas you can use to meet people you want in your crew. I've also included places where you could network for information and opportunities.

1. **Form a success group.** We've already covered this, but I believe this is something that you should begin working on now. Continue thinking about potential members and add them to the outline you created earlier.

2. **Find a mentor.** If you know someone that is doing well, ask that person to become your mentor. If they are a straight A student or a great student athlete, perhaps you can shadow this person to see what their day looks like. Observe how they study or what their workout regime is like. Once you find a mentor, possibly their success group or network could become a part of your network.

3. **Call Clubs and Organizations.** The Boys and Girls Club of America offer many different programs on education, careers, character, leadership, health, and life skills. Call your local club to see what they offer for your age group. Here's a tip: if an organization cannot provide help for you, **always** ask if they know of any other organizations that might provide the service you are looking for.

4. **Contact your local YMCA.** This is another community-based organization you can call for information on classes or other groups.

5. **Join a church group.** If family or friends attend church, ask if their church has a program or support group that might assist you.

These are a few ideas that can help you as you surround yourself with people who are looking to improve their lives by checking their crew.

This is the end of round three. Please take time to review all the things you have taken away from this round. Make it a point to share those things with someone else.

NOTES

ROUND FOUR
REACH FURTHER

When someone tells you that your arms are too short to reach for the stars, tell that person, "That's why stars fall!"

-Ian J. Humphrey

Reaching further is simply doing more today than you did yesterday. It's being satisfied with where you are in life but refusing to stop there, because you know you can achieve more.

Examples: If your goal today is to read one chapter of this book, tomorrow challenge yourself to read two chapters. If you decided to study for an exam coming up in a week, study for one hour today, and increase the time tomorrow.

After I decided to change my life and focus on success, I began to take every class that the prison offered. These classes included life skills, anger management, computer classes, writing classes, journaling courses, and more. I completed each one, learning as much as I could from those classes.

After completing a class, I would immediately enroll in it again. If it was full, then I would put myself on the waiting list. Why did I do this? Because after taking the course, I was a different person. I knew that by taking the course again, I would walk away with knowledge I had not seen the first time.

As you begin to grow and change, your perspective on life will also change. You will no longer see things the same way you once did,

REACHING FURTHER IS DELIBERATELY MAKING THE DECISION TO IMPROVE A LITTLE EACH DAY.

Has anyone ever said that you're not smart enough to go to college, you're not athletic enough to play that sport, or no one from this neighborhood has ever become successful? When others say those things, what they are essentially saying is your arms aren't long enough to reach for the stars. They are telling you to stop dreaming, because your dreams will never become a reality. The quote at the beginning of this chapter says to tell that person, "That's why stars fall." This means if you are willing to work hard, search high and low, take the extra steps that many are too lazy to take, while ignoring all the naysayers, you will find the star that has fallen just for you. As long as you believe, refuse to quit, and want it bad enough, *you* can achieve almost anything you set your mind to.

THE PERSISTENCE OF AN ANT

We have a flowerbed in the front of our home. During the summer months, ants tunnel to the surface.

The summer my son was six years old, he became fascinated with ants. He would keep himself busy for hours trying to stop them with a small branch he had found in our yard. One time he relentlessly followed one ant. He placed the branch in its path hoping the ant would crawl onto it. Finally, he became frustrated when the ant crawled around, underneath, and over the branch. I was amused as I sat on our front porch watching my son. After a while, he stopped, looked up at me, and asked, "Dad, where are they going, and why won't they stop?" I explained how each ant had a job to do. If they stopped, it would prevent them from succeeding with their assignment.

After my explanation, I watched him mentally process what I had said. Without any warning, he turned and he began stomping the ground in an unsuccessful attempt to kill the ants.

When it comes to achieving your goals, do you have the persistence of an ant? Are you unwilling to stop until you complete the task at hand?

When you set out to achieve your goals, there will be obstacles, people will try to stomp on your dreams and impede your progress. Just like the ant, you must be so focused and set on achieving your goals that you are willing to go over, underneath, around, and, in some cases, through any obstacles. Unless you are willing to relentlessly pursue your goals, then reaching for the stars is simply a cliché.

While in prison, I listened to many offenders as they spoke about changing their lives. I watched them walk out of prison only to return a few months later. Why? The old saying is true: talk is cheap and doesn't lead to change. *Action* is what leads to change. It's easy to say, "I'm going to reach for the stars." But when it's time to start reaching, that's where most people fall short. They become distracted and divert their attention and energy on things that do not move them toward their goals. That's why it's important to create an Action Plan!

Earlier, you should have written the things you envision doing in the future. You should have started an Action Plan from the Now and Then Process™ that you worked on in chapter one. These are tools that will help you reach your destination.

The following is an example of how I took my goals and the Now and Then Process™ to create an action plan.

When I decided that I wanted to become a better speaker and possibly begin speaking professionally, I wrote the goal down in my own journal using the Now and Then Process™.

BETTER SPEAKER- PROFESSIONAL SPEAKER
GOAL

Now--THEN
Join Toastmasters to improve speaking skills.

NOW---THEN
Contact schools and offer to speak.

NOW--THEN
Find a mentor.

Here's what the road to accomplishing this goal using the Now and Then Process™ looked like: I gave myself one week to complete the task of finding a Toastmasters club. I needed to act quickly—I knew if I waited, it was very likely I would never do it. I used my computer to find a club that met weekly and was close to my house. I called the president of that club for more information. At their next meeting, I was there.

*(Toastmasters is an educational organization that operates clubs worldwide for the purpose of helping people improve their communication and leadership skills.)

Toastmasters can help you do the following:

- Become a confident communicator
- Teach you to give powerful presentations
- Hone management skills

- Helps you accept criticism, allowing you to improve
- Develop leadership skills

All of these skills gave me the confidence and tools needed to move up within the business world.

Secret: One of the top three fears of people is speaking in public. If you conquer that fear by developing your speaking skills, you will have a competitive edge in the job market.

I made the commitment and attended Toastmasters meetings every week for one year. I studied and applied all of the new things I was learning to my personal and professional life.

Two months later, right on schedule, I contacted a youth organization to schedule my first presentation. Shortly thereafter, I gave my first professional speech. Two months after the speech, I found a mentor who I communicated with regularly, professional speaker Ty Howard. I visited his websites many times and watched several of his videos on You Tube. I sent him an email and explained that I needed any advice or instruction that he could offer. From there a friendship/mentorship was born. Prior to Toastmasters, I never would have had the courage to take these initiatives.

I continue to write out my goals, and use the Now and Then Process™ to see them through.

Write down a few things where you can use the Now and Then Process™ to accomplish.

EVERY TIME YOU RAISE THE BAR, YOU SET A NEW STANDARD.

After you blow up a balloon, it can never return to its original shape. I look at personal development the same way: After each new accomplishment, you raise the bar. You have now created a new standard by which you must continue to live. You should refuse to return to the person you were before gaining new knowledge. Never lower the bar or your standard after you have raised it. To do so is to move backwards, which is not the direction you wish to go.

Two years after joining the Toastmasters organization, I decided to compete in the annual Toastmasters International Speech Contest. Every year over 30,000 Toastmasters enter the competition. Many enter with the hope of being crowned the next World Champion of

Public Speaking. Others simply enter to challenge their own personal achievement and development.

The competition spans over a six-month period. Each contestant prepares and delivers a short speech in front of an audience. The contest requires many hours of writing and practicing your speech.

In 2010, I took the challenge and entered the competition. In preparation for the contests, I would practice my seven-minute speech twenty to thirty times a day. In the end, I was one of nine speakers who advanced to compete on the championship stage. Although I did not win, it was a tremendous experience that required me to raise my own bar on personal achievement. The competition is my new standard, and I will continue to compete when possible.

Doing more requires constant reminders in order to continue pushing yourself to achieve more.

Below, I have created reminders using the alphabet that will help you push yourself to new heights. I suggest you copy these and hang them in a place to serve as extra motivation.

REACHING FURTHER A-Z

A. Align yourself with successful and positive people.

B. Believe in yourself and your potential.

C. Create and set deadlines for your goals.

D. Delete all negative contacts from your life.

E. Enjoy success no matter how small.

F. Forgive others and yourself.

G. Give more than people expect you to.

H. Have and maintain faith.

I. Improve strained relationships. Ignore the words of negative and toxic people.

J. Just do it. Procrastination is a dream buster!

K. Knowledge is power. Enroll, learn, and repeat.

L. Learn to love yourself first.

M. Maintain a positive attitude in spite of your surroundings and conditions.

N. Never underestimate yourself.

O. Observe the habits of successful people, and apply them to your own life.

P. Practice being the person you wish to become.

Q. Quitting is not an option.

R. Read more often.

S. Step out of your comfort zone.

T. Trust someone enough to share your dreams.

U. Understand that difficult times are only temporary.

V. Visualize success in all you do.

W. Work harder today than you did yesterday.

X. Xerox and place copies of your goals where you can see them.

Y. You control your own destiny.

Z. Zero in and accomplish one goal at a time.

I challenge you and your success group to memorize each letter and what it stands for. Use them to remind each other to reach further.

This is the end of round four. Please take time to reflect on the things you have taken away from this round. Make it a point to share those things with someone else.

NOTES

_____

_____

_____

_____

_____

_____

_____

_____

_____

_____

_____

_____

ROUND FIVE
TALK TO YOURSELF

*"I began telling myself I was the greatest be-
fore I believed that I really was."*

-Muhammad Ali

Do you have a nickname that you answer to? And if so, what does it say about you?

Growing up in L.A., I knew many of my neighborhood friends only by their nicknames: Stormy Weather, No Luv, Monkey Man and Cutthroat. The problem with these names, is once you accept them, it is easy to live down to or up to the nickname given to you by someone else. So, be aware of what you allow yourself to be called.

The Greatest is the nickname of the legendary boxer Muhammad Ali. Do you know who declared Ali *The Greatest*? As stated in the previous quote, he did! Many believed Muhammad Ali was a trash talker. This was evident by an additional nickname given to him, which was *The Louisville Lip*.

I believe when Ali began *talking trash,* he wasn't really speaking to the public, or his opponent; I believe he was talking to *himself.* No matter what the public says, no one can ever become the greatest unless they themselves believe it first. Ali, while appearing cocky and arrogant, was simply convincing himself that he could win.

If you say something to yourself enough times, positive or negative, sooner or later you will believe it. Once you believe it, then you will set out to prove it.

After talking to himself repeatedly and convincing himself he was the greatest, Ali set out to prove it. He was so confident that he would call the round in which his opponent would fall. He believed in his words; so, once the fight began, the only thing left was to take action.

After hearing all of the negative things I was destined to become, I unconsciously repeated the words of others to myself. Eventually, I believed them. Deep down a part of me easily accepted my prison sentence. After hearing those negative words so many times, I believed and visualized myself in prison years before it actually happened. Had I known that I could cancel out the negative words of others simply by speaking positive words to myself, my life would have taken a different path.

The most important things you will
hear today will be the things you say to yourself!

What are you saying to yourself daily? You must realize that your words have power! Have you ever thought to yourself, *I can't get anything right,* or *I'm so stupid!* There is a way you can reverse those thoughts in your mind.

Begin and end each day with a positive affirmation. Starting to-morrow, as soon as your feet hit the floor say this to yourself, *It's A Great Day To Be Alive*! Saying this should serve as a reminder that someone else wasn't so lucky and that you've been given an oppor-tunity to do something **remarkable**!

Often times we wake up and begin our day focusing on all that is wrong and not giving any thought to all of our blessings. Although your circumstances may not be what you wished, you have oppor-tunities that would not exist if you were not here.

I can recall my grandmother waking up each day and saying, "Lord, thank you for allowing me to see another day." She said this even louder on the days we were without food and didn't know from where our next meal would come. Now I realize that she was beginning her day on a positive note, dictating and calling forth the type of day she wished to have. She was talking to herself!

Have you ever heard the saying "Did you get up on the wrong side of the bed this morning?" Well, the wrong side of the bed is the negative side. If the first thing you say to yourself every day is negative, then you set yourself up to see only that for the entire day. This will cause you to miss opportunities, because *you* have conditioned yourself to do so.

It's important to monitor your self-talk and to make sure it isn't negative. If it is, then being aware of it is the first step in correcting this self-destructive problem. A friend of mine placed a rubber band on his wrist to correct his issues with negative self-talk. Every time he caught negative thoughts creeping into his mind, he snapped the rubber band. Over time, he no longer needed to snap the rubber band, because he had trained his mind to subconsciously do it for him.

Find a constructive way to correct yourself whenever you find that your thoughts are bringing you down.

Earlier I talked about Mr. Lyles telling me he believed in me, and he knew I could get out of prison and do great things. I wrote about looking at my reflection in the mirror and repeating his words to myself. What I did not mention is that this became a ritual for me. For so many years, while growing up, I repeated someone else's negative words to my reflection. However, this time the words I repeated were positive. I made it a point, especially when my thoughts were negative, to repeat Mr. Lyles's words as many times as I could throughout the day: "Mr. Lyles believes in you, and you can do *great* things."

Over time, Mr. Lyles's words became my very own words as I began to change the negative image I had of myself. Positive thoughts became the norm for me. However, when a negative thought did creep in, I noticed it right away and forced it out of my mind by replacing it with positivity.

EXERCISE

On a sheet of paper, track all your negative thoughts throughout the day, and write them down. If it isn't possible to write them down, track them by number and write down the total number of negative thoughts. Try to decrease this number each day. You can make a game of it. Meet with your success group at the end of each day to see how many negative thoughts they had. See who has begun to decrease that number.

Begin taking small corrective actions each time you have a negative thought by instantly replacing it with a positive thought. Muhammad Ali yelled, "I'm The Greatest!"

EXERCISE:

Practice saying the following Muhammad Ali quotes out loud to yourself and with your success group.

- "I'm The Greatest!"
- "I'm the double greatest!"
- "It's not bragging if you can back it up!"
- "If you dream of beating me, you better wake up and apologize!"

You can use these or come up with your own saying. Whatever you decide, use your saying to begin each day to push those negative thoughts out of your mind.

THIRTY PERCENTER

"Seventy percent of you losers will be back!" Prison Guard

During my incarceration, the recidivism rate In California was 70%. That meant that for every 10 people released, 7 of them would return to prison. It was common for a prison guard to yell, "Seventy percent of you losers will be back!" The first time I heard this statement, I became nervous and wondered whether or not I could beat the odds. I remember thinking, *70% … I don't have a chance*! But with the power of self-talk, I learned to look at the bright side of this horrendous statistic. Instead of focusing on the 70% that returned, I began to focus on the 30% who did not. I started calling myself a "30 Percenter." I would look in the mirror and repeat those words to myself over and over again: "**You are a 30 Percenter!**" I placed myself in the 30% that would never return to prison, and I focused on it. Anytime a guard spoke the words, "Seventy percent of you losers will be back," I countered those words with my own: "**I am a Thirty Percenter: I ain't never coming back!**"

We don't often look for the positive side of a negative situation. The statistic was frightening. There wasn't anything I could do to change it other than focusing on the things I could control. It is important that no matter what the odds are, you must place yourself on the side that is victorious and successful. Say it out loud over and over again, and then begin to take the necessary action to ensure that you are the victor.

BURY THE WHY TRY ATTITUDE!

When it comes to trying new things, negative attitudes will kill our chances of success before we ever start. For instance: "I'm not going to get paroled my first time up, so *why try*?" This is a form of speaking negatively to yourself. You've killed your chances before ever starting. When you lack belief, it shows. The people who surround you will not only see it but also feel the negative energy that comes from that type of attitude.

By training yourself to have positive thoughts on a regular basis, you will begin to see the possibilities. This is what will give your life meaning. Over time, your thoughts will become more like *I may not get an A the first semester; however, I'm going to do everything within my power and control to make it happen. If I don't reach my goal this time, I will make some changes and continue to work hard.*

GO FOR IT ANYWAY!

Have you ever watched a football team that is down by one touchdown with 80 yards to go? Even though they have only a few seconds left on the clock, do they attempt one last play? Why do they line up for a Hail Mary pass even though their fans start to leave as if the game was over? They do it because of the possibilities. If the pass is unsuccessful, they can walk off the field knowing they gave their all until the final second. It would be impossible to win that game if the players or coaches had the *Why Try Attitude*. Be aware of that outlook and replace it with *Why Not Try*!

There will be times when you will face a long shot or extreme odds, but *why not try* is the question you should ask yourself. What do you have to lose by trying? Absolutely nothing!

This is the end of round five. Please take time to review the things you have taken away from this round. Make it a point to share those things with someone.

NOTES

DON'T GIVE UP

You're going to make it: just don't quit!

DON'T QUIT!

When things go wrong, as they sometimes will,
When the road you're trudging seems all uphill,
When the funds are low and the debts are high,
And you want to smile but you have to sigh,
When care is pressing you down a bit
Rest if you must, but don't you quit.
For life is queer with its twists and turns,
As every one of us sometimes learns,
And many a failure turns about,
When he might have won if he'd stuck it out.
Success is just failure turned inside out,
The silver tint of the clouds of doubt.
And you never can tell how close you are,

It may be near when it seems so far.
So stick to the fight when you're hardest hit,
It's when things seem worst that YOU MUST NOT QUIT!
-Anonymous

While in prison, my desire to succeed was very strong. However, there were many days I wanted to give up. I had my goals written down, and I would talk to myself every day. I had a vision of what I wanted, but still there were days where those things just did not seem like enough! This is what I've learned: **This is normal** when you have a goal worth achieving; a goal worth fighting for!

I had many good days when I believed I would succeed, accomplish my dream of getting out of prison, and live a productive life. However, without fail, the tough days returned and forced me to question myself and whether I was strong enough to survive.

I began thinking about giving up. I felt as though staying on the path that would free me from prison was too difficult. When those days came, I held on by reading my goals and maintaining my belief that if others did it, then so could I. I grasped on to anything that would strengthen my belief in myself to succeed. I confided in my accountability partners. I tried whatever it took to force those negative thoughts out of my mind. I flooded my mind with pictures of my hopes and my dreams.

Have you ever thought about giving up?

The day I stepped from behind those barbed wire fences, I returned home to my family feeling triumphant as though I had accomplished the impossible. Little did I know that the real battle had just begun.

Again I heard the voices, "You'll never amount too much! You'll return to prison!" While searching for a job, I heard a new voice: "We cannot hire you!" Once again, doubts and thoughts of giving up crept back into my mind. However, I had trained myself to combat those negative voices. I was determined not to let them get the best of me! "**This is normal,**" I told myself.

When *you* least expect it, when things are going well, something is going to happen that will make you question yourself. Thoughts of giving up will creep into your mind. It doesn't matter how bad you want something or how long you've prepared for that moment, self-doubt will begin to set in. Know and expect for this to happen, and be prepared. Make the commitment right now that when those thoughts knock on your door, you will continue to fight for the things you want in life.

Why do people give up on their goals and dreams?

No one thinks about giving up when things are going great. *This is too hard!* or *I can't go on!* doesn't enter into our minds when everything is going as planned. It's only when things get tough that you consider quitting. The days when you aren't seeing results fast enough is when you may think about quitting. Be patient and know that if you continue on the path you have laid for yourself and stay consistent, you will see results.

I remember going to the gym for the first time. After my workout, I went home, took my shirt off, and began flexing in a mirror. I was already looking for results ... *after only one hour at the gym*! This is the wrong mentality when you truly want to become successful. In today's society, we often expect results at a lightning fast pace. There's a saying that says it takes 20 years to become an overnight success! This simply means that it's going to take time and a lot of hard work.

You will not become a better basketball player because you went out into your driveway *one* time and shot a few layups. If you are struggling in math or science, your grades will not change if you stay up one night trying to cram your head full of information. Practicing and studying must become a habit, and it must be repeated over and over again if you are to see positive results. Positive results require sacrifice. This is where the road gets rough and many people think about giving up. This is where you will need to remind yourself of the tools I have given you.

Don't compare yourself with others!

When you compare yourself to others, you risk believing that they have some unique gift of knowledge or intelligence that you do not possess: "She's smarter than I am. He's faster and stronger than I am!" Instead of comparing yourself to someone else, commit to putting in the necessary work to get better.

Look at the things you want to achieve in your life; it's always a good idea to find someone that is already successful in that area. If possible, contact them, and ask what it took for them to reach their goals. Ask about the hardships or challenges they faced along the way.

You will find a very successful person who appears to have effortlessly succeeded at anything they touch. You won't see what it took for them to get to where they are. You won't see the late nights, the sweat, and the tears of frustration before they *made it*! You won't see the hard work they continue to put in to maintain that level of success.

Being unwilling to maintain a regime for success can lead to quitting.

Success is like that first car you bought. You worked hard and finally had enough to buy it. It's nice and shiny with a newly vacuumed interior, and you're smiling from ear to ear as you drive it off of the car lot. Making sure no one scratches it, you park your new car a mile away from other cars. You give your car a name, and no one is allowed to eat inside or touch the outside with greasy hands. It's important that your new car maintains its shine!

However, over time, you realize you must wash and wax it, put gas in it, and get the engine tuned up in order to keep it running and looking smooth. If you're not willing to put in the maintenance, the shine will quickly fade, and your car will inevitably quit running.

When it comes to success, you must work very hard to achieve it; however, once you get it, it becomes even harder to maintain.

There is not a man or a woman alive who has not thought about giving up. If you think about successful athletes and entertainers, at some point in their life they have hit tough times that forced them to consider giving up. We *do not* know the names of the ones who gave up. However, those who refused to give up, their names are known worldwide.

On those days when you feel like giving up, remember that **you are not alone**! Will you be one of those that yearn for it bad enough that you will find a reason to continue the fight?

EXERCISE

Take a moment and think about all the things you want to accomplish in your life. Use the list below to write down some of the reasons you will refuse to quit until you accomplish your goals.

This is the end of the sixth and final round. You can now raise your hands in victory!

Please take the time to reflect on all the things you have taken away from this round. Make it a point to share those things with someone else.

NOTES

THE DECISION

After every great fight, if no one has been knocked out, the judges add up points to decide on a winner.

Every day you will face the biggest and baddest opponent you will ever face: **Yourself**. At the end of each day, you have to make a decision on whether or not you honestly feel that you did enough to win the round that day. Here's the beauty of being your greatest opponent: **you** decide whether or not **you** refuse to make excuses. *You* decide whether or not *you* will take chances. *You* decide whether or not *you* will check your crew. *You* decide whether or not *you* will reach further and do what is necessary to achieve your goals. *You* decide whether or not *you* will speak life into your dreams by talking to yourself. *You* decide whether or not to give up. *You* and *you* alone get to decide! Keep reaching, keep battling, and keep going. If you get knocked down, remember: ***It's not about the knockdown; it's about the get up!*** *It's about what you do **after** the knockdown which defines who you are!*

THOSE DECISIONS ARE YOURS!

NOTES

Don't forget to look me up on:
Instagram
You-Tube
Facebook
Pinerest
Twitter

BOOK IAN TO SPEAK AT YOUR EVENT
Find out how at www.beianspired.com

Made in the USA
San Bernardino, CA
20 May 2014